I'd like to dedicate the communication videos and workbook to all of my students, past and present. I'd like to thank my colleagues, administrators, friends and family for their constant support. May everyone who uses this book learn quickly!

Janet Scarpone

Learn Oral Communication Quickly
Workbook

Learn Quickly
P.O. Box 336
Boulder, CO 80306-0336
1-888-LRN-FAST

ISBN 1-889434-35-3

TABLE OF CONTENTS

Communication Basics
plus
How to Get
Over
the Fear
of
Public Speaking

A. Communications Basics

Now that you've watched Video 1, please answer the following questions in your own words.

1. What is communication? How do we communicate?

2. What are some interesting communication experiences you have had?

3. What makes a good speaker?

4. Whose voice do you like to listen to and why?

5. What makes a good listener? How can you become a better listener?

6. When can listening be a matter of life and death?

7. How can you be a good audience member?

8. How do we breathe? What is proper breathing for speech?

9. What can you do to improve your breathing?

10. What can you do to improve your public speaking ability?

B. Getting over the fear: breathing and relaxing

- Practice breathing fully and deeply every day.

- Extend your exhalations daily by counting numbers, saying oh, reciting the alphabet, or timing yourself. See if every day your exhalations can be just a bit longer.

- Pull your abdomen in for that last gush of air to last a bit longer.

- Tell yourself often, "I can do it. I can speak well in front of a group." Believe in yourself.

- Change the fear into excitement.

- Practice a lot.

- Tense and release the muscles in your body to totally relax.

- Visualize yourself in public speaking situations doing an outstanding job.

- Visualize the audience enjoying every word you have to say.

C. **Let's begin to practice oral communication with storytelling.**

This is a simple exercise which you can do at a party, at school, with co-workers during break time, with friends in social situations, and, of course, during a speech.

Think of something that has happened to you in the present or past that is interesting. Make sure the story has a beginning, a middle and an end. Make sure it has a moral or a point. Rather than write it down, practice it out loud, over and over until you are comfortable. Perhaps you can watch yourself in a mirror or record yourself on audio or videotape. Do practice out loud, not just in your mind. Actually say the words so that your mouth becomes comfortable with your story. Practice out loud, to your cat, dog, husband, neighbor, friend; make sure it's a friendly audience!

Practice until you know it and feel comfortable. The more you practice, the more you can concentrate on performance techniques like:

- Eye contact - really look at each person.

- Posture - stand up straight.

- Appropriate hand gestures - let your hands talk, too, but not too much!

- Enough volume - people want to hear you, but not too loud.

- Enthusiasm - help your audience "feel" your story.

- Stay in one place - no pacing around.

- Timing - short and sweet (2-3 minutes).

- Avoid crutch phrases - like, um, ugh, you know.

Remember to pick an interesting story. Here are some suggestions.
Perhaps you can pick something that happened to you while: at school, at
work, on vacation, at a job interview, at an important meeting, catching the
bus or train.

How to Demonstrate, Introduce, and Make a Toast

A. Demonstration Speaking

What would you like to teach others to do?

What would you like to demonstrate?

What would you like to see demonstrated?

Pick something you like doing, you know how to do, and you can feel comfortable doing.   Here are some demonstration topics:

- How to bake a cake
- How to wash a car
- How to pop popcorn
- How to use a blender, VCR, cuisinart, electric razor, ATM machine, vacuum, etc.
- How to chop onions
- How to wash windows
- How to change a tire
- How to play a sport (show how to do one activity) e.g. a serve in tennis, ping pong, volleyball or badmitton; a golf swing; a foul shot in basketball
- How to make salsa
- How to make a dessert, appetizer, main meal - some kind of food
- How to do origami
- How to sign
- How to peel and eat a mango
- How to make sushi
- How to chop vegetables
- How to make vegetable decorations
- How to make knots
- How to play cards
- How to make a fruit smoothie
- How to diaper a baby
- How to set a table
- How to use chopsticks
- How to fill out an application
- How to make a resume

B. Outlining

How many parts to a speech?

After you pick a topic, begin to fill out the outline form. Remember to practice from the outline to give your speech an extemporaneous quality rather than write it out word for word.

Demonstration Speech Outline

1. **Introduction**

   a. **Attention getter**

   b. **Introduce the topic to the audience**

   c. **Purpose of your speech**

2. **Body**

   a. **History and/or importance**

      1) **Facts that support the purpose**

      2) **Examples**

   b. **Demonstration**

3. **Conclusion**

   a. **Restate the purpose of your speech**

   b. **Recap the demonstration**

   c. **Make a concluding statement**

C. Introductions

Tips

What kind of person is this?

What is the person's background?

What is important about the person?

What will he or she be saying?

What is he or she known for?

How do you feel about him or her?

Make it short, sweet and believable.

Don't oversell the speaker!

Perhaps mention a short anecdote from the speaker's life.

Mention his or her background and/or expertise.

Mention things done by the speaker in the past.

Using what you know about introductions, make up an introduction for your favorite movie stars speaking about the following topics:

How to memorize easily and quickly

How to audition well

How to saddle a horse

How to use a sword

How to build muscles

How to creatively discipline children

How to run for political office

How to direct a scene in a movie

How to make a lot of money

How to prepare a gourmet meal

How to lose weight

How to gain weight

How to be a star

D. Toastmaking

Keep it short and sweet!

Prepare.

Make it apropos to the situation.

Make it interesting.

Let it hit the spot.

Make a toast for a:

Birthday	Promotion
Wedding	Holiday Dinner
Graduation	Successful Venture
Birth	First Car
Engagement	Vacation
New Job	First Child

How to Persuade, Answer Questions, and Accept Awards

A. Persuasive Speaking

1. What is persuasion?

2. What is ethos?

3. What is pathos?

4. What is logos?

5. How do advertisers use ethos, pathos and logos in specific advertisements?

B. What would you like to be persuaded to do? What would you like to persuade others to do?

Pick a topic for a persuasive speech. Pick something you believe in. Here are some topic ideas:

Stop smoking	Travel
Eat more vegetables	Learn another language
Go to school	Dance
Go on vacation	Volunteer
Eat healthy foods	Believe in yourself
Exercise	Play sports
Study	Study computers
Read more books	Use the internet
Use your imagination	Start your own business
Think positive	Speak in public
Buy a car	Go back to school
Use public transportation	

C. Outlining

After you pick a topic, begin to fill out the outline form. Remember to include ethos, pathos, and logos. Use testimony of authority, personal examples, facts and statistics as proof. Remember to practice from the outline to give your speech an extemporaneous quality rather than writing it out word for word.

Also, list persuasive words and phrases that support and or convince listeners.

Basic Speech Outline

I. **Introduction**
   a. **Attention getter**
   b. **Introduce the topic to the audience**
   c. **Purpose of your speech**

II. **Body**
   a. **Main point 1**
      1. **Explain it**
      2. **Prove it**

   b. **Main point 2**
      1. **Explain it**
      2. **Prove it**

   c. **Main point 3**
      1. **Explain it**
      2. **Prove it**

III. **Conclusion**
   a. **Restate the purpose of your speech**
   b. **Recap the main points**
   c. **Make a concluding statement**

D.   Answering Questions

- "I have a few minutes for questions" or "I look forward to answering your questions."

- Always rephrase the question: "The question is _____."

- Rephrase a hostile question as a positively-toned question.

- Share your eye contact with the rest of the audience while answering the question.

- Never argue.

- "I have time for one more question" or "Who will ask the last question?"

Troubleshoot by thinking of various easy and difficult questions the audience might ask for each of the persuasive topics (including your own) listed in this chapter. How would you answer them?

E.   Accepting an Award

- Be enthusiastic

- Use a positive statement

- Be joyful

- Thank appropriate people - but not everyone in the world

- Keep it short and sweet

- Make it interesting

- Practice

- Prepare

- Smile

- Be sincere and grateful!

Imagine several awards you would like to win. What will you say when you receive them?

How
to
Read Aloud

A. Vocal Improvement

1. Read this paragraph twice - make it sound boring.

    Then make it sound interesting.

    "It was a long, long time ago. The young couple knew it was time to move on to yet another crowded village. They felt sad and angry. Times had been, and still were, so difficult. They needed to find work because their children were hungry. What else could they do?"

    What did you do differently with each reading?

2. Say the following words and see if you can express the meaning of each word as you say it.

large	fast	slow	tiny	sexy
hot	baby	quiet	cute	light
cool	beautiful	calm	stupid	heavy

3. Look in the mirror while you do this: Show the following emotions on your face and in your voice as you say the words with feeling.

thankfulness   worry   anger   joy   wonder

fear   infatuation   disgust   love   surprise

4. Pausing

Read both paragraphs aloud and pause at the slash marks. Which paragraph sounds better?

The/kitten/yawned/and/then/walked/to/the/window./Looking/outside/
the/little/kitten/saw/hundreds/of/tiny/snowflakes/falling/in/the/sky./
The/back/yard/was/already/covered/with/snow./ When/would/it/stop?

The kitten yawned/and then walked to the window./ Looking outside/
the little kitten saw hundreds of tiny snowflakes/falling in the sky./ The
back yard was already covered with snow./ When would it stop?/

5. Volume

Read each sentence out loud. The first time you read it, read it loudly - very loud! The second time, read it softly - very softly!

I love you.
Don't buy that.
Careful!
What did you say?
I don't believe you.
Where are you going?
Don't say that.
Did you hear me?
Are you sure?
Let's go!

In what types of situations would you say each of these sentences loudly?

Softly?

What happens to the meaning of the sentence when you change the volume?

6. Say the following phrases three times showing anger, fear and joy as you do:

Aren't you finished?
What did you say?
No way.
Is that right?
You don't say?
Yes, I will.
No, I won't
You did what?
You must be kidding?
Control yourself.

7. Please say the following words expressing the opposite meaning e.g. say "yes" when you mean "no".

yes   quick
no   slow
happy   good
sad   evil
love   hate

8. Read the following sentences aloud:

I would like to eat dinner now.

Did you sleep well?

Take them away.

How are you feeling?

Mind your own business.

Try reading these sentences as if you were:

A troubled teenager   A frustrated child

A contented grandparent   An angry cab driver

A famous opera singer   An award winning student

A sick child   A busy veterinarian

A mad scientist   A loving parent

9. Read aloud:

"I believe you are correct."

Read it as if you were:

A nervous middle-aged secretary

A scared six-year-old boy

A kindly old neighbor

An angry customer

A very smart instructor

10. Rate

Read aloud the following sentences. Read each very quickly and then very slowly. Which sounds better?

I need you.

Where are you going?

Help me now.

Are you ready to go?

What's the rush?

You must be kidding!

I don't believe you.

What did you say?

Let's do it now!

I see you.

B.   Practice Imagining - Daydreaming - Visualizing

Think about:

Your ideal vacation

Your favorite meal

A date with your favorite movie star

A perfect day

A perfect night

A successful encounter

A picnic in the country

An afternoon at the beach

A special birthday celebration

What you'd do with a winning lottery ticket

The house of your dreams

Skiing

Swimming

Playing your favorite sport

Your ideal family

C. Oral Interpretation of Literature

What kinds of books do you like to read?

Do you like poetry? Drama?

Go back in your memory to books you have read. What did you like? Pick a short selection (1 or 2 pages) from a novel, short story, book of poetry or a play. Analyze it first with these questions:

1. What is the point of view?

   1st person - I, my, me, we, ours, us

   2nd person - you, yours

   3rd person - he, she, it, they, them, theirs

2. Who is speaking?

   Who has the writer created to say these words?

   Who is saying the words?

   What does the speaker look like?

   Is it a man or woman?

   Old or young?

   Tall or short?

   Educated or not educated?

   Working or unemployed?

   What kind of job?

   What would the speaker eat for breakfast?

   Where would she/he go on vacation?

   What kinds of clothes would he/she wear?

3. To whom is the speaker talking? Self? Others?

4. When is the speaker speaking?

   Spring? Summer? Fall? Winter?

   1950? 1980? 2010? Now?

   Morning? Afternoon? Evening?

5. Where is he/she speaking?

   Inside or outside?

   Which room?

   What country?

6. What kinds of feelings is the speaker expressing?

   How can you tell?

D   Putting It All Together

After you have analyzed the piece, copy it over in an easy-to-read format - use big letters! Use a music stand or hold the black binder with your script enclosed in your hand. Practice - practice - practice. Read it many, many times imagining yourself as the speaker(s). Listen to yourself - tape yourself - videotape yourself. Listen. Have you captured the essence of the piece? What about your tone of voice? Have you varied your rate and intensity? Are the words and feelings understandable? Are you pausing in the right places? Are you emphasizing the right words? Are you building pictures in other people's minds when you read? How's your volume and intensity - appropriate? Are you relaying the mood of the piece? Ask others for their opinions. Make sure you have picked an interesting selection. Give it an appropriate introduction. Keep your selection short at first. Then experiment with long pieces. Have fun!!

Here are some pieces of literature. Analyze them and practice for performance.
Rate yourself with the questions above!

Me An' Six Foot Sam
by Jeanette Adams

Ole big mouf Bessie
went an' tole my daddy
i wuz drinkin' peach wine
wid a boy from town

dat big mouf heifer
musta been hot 'cause
it wuzn't her under de dogwood tree
just me an'
six foot Sam

my daddy wuz mad
wouldn't speak to me
for a good while
then came askin'
where i got dem flowers from
shoot
i picked 'em from de field
and put 'em in dat green jug

now i'm sho' glad he didn'
ask me where i got de jug.

six foot Sam
give it to me
after we finished de wine
Lord ha' mercy
dat man is fine

got hair all up
under his chin
big straight teeth
wid an easy grin

ole raisin eyes
an' a bulldog nose
he's right clean
but don't fuss 'bout clothes

hands so long
you gotta hold 'em
so bold you gotta help 'em
lips so loud
you gotta kiss 'em

ole six foot Sam
is a mighty fine man

i guess he better ask my daddy
fo' dis young gal's han'

AT THE TOWN MEETING

by Jeanette Adams

the man had come
a long way
with his wife

the boy had come
a long way
with his mother

the man who was 71
did not know the boy
who was 8

after waiting for hours
the boy saw the man
walk onstage in a dark suit
eyes folded into
his warm brown face

the boy in the dark sweater
stood and cheered
with the crowd

the man spoke
quietly, carefully
refusing to be drawn
away from his message

the boy listened
eyes wide
in his smooth brown face
hoping to ask his question

the host called him last
the boy spoke
clearly, simply
wanting to know
how could he help

the man smiled
the crowd clapped
the host invited the boy onstage

the man requested paper
the boy vaulted over the edge
halted by the chair
the man wrote a note

to Bernard L. Charles, III
from Nelson R. Mandela

the boy smiled
the man stood
with his left arm
around the boy
his right fist
raised in salute
the crowd roared
the interview ended

the boy will never forget
the man's courage

the man will never forget
the boy's concern

THE DINOSAUR SEES THE RAINBOW

The dinosaur left his jungle house
And walked to Onekahaha Beach
The silver dinosaur was dying to swim
He jumped in the water
And the waves pushed him back
He was sad and started to grumble
He sat down in the water and a rock poked his tail
He jumped out and looked up to the sky
And saw the rainbow
It was pretty and soft and colorful
There was red and orange, yellow and blue
There was even lavender and green!
It was the most spectacular rainbow he'd ever seen!
He watched until it faded away
Then walked back home smiling all the way

Jeanette Adams and Miss Evelyn's Class
The Good Years Pre-School
Hilo, Hawaii, 1984

CONTRIBUTOR

Jeanette Adams holds a MA in Creative Writing from The City College of New York. Her poetry has appeared in numerous publications including *Essence, The Amsterdam News, and Keeping the Faith*: *Writing by Contemprary Black American Women.* Jeanette has written three books: *Sukari, Picture Me in a Poem, and Love Lyrics.*

WOUNDED CHILD
by Jan Lee Ande

She wants to be heard. She waits, patient
as earth, tilling her garden of memories.
Her plants grow tall: thyme, forget-me-not,
passion flower, chokeweed.

She catches tears in hollowed hands,
lets the salt leach out. Soon there is water
for dousing, each tended plant giving itself
to form, each seed grasping its destiny.

You might think hers is a solitary life,
yet she has an abundance of company,
child after child in gardens of tangle and rue.

They stand, bare faces to the sun, stunned
and never aging. They remain seven,
eight, thirteen, forever, with knobby knees
and toothy smiles, among the stalks
and leaves, sighing.

WORLD TREE
by Jan Lee Ande

If you are lost in the world, bewildered
in the middle ground between heaven
and earth, come stand here. Say: sequoia,
redwood, banyan. Say: *El Gigante* and
bristlecone pine.

Take off your shoes. Let the moist soil
rise between your toes. Your feet
are rootstock and seedling. Listen to wise
words thrummed in sap and bark.

Capture daylight in your branches.
Green leaves tendril from your crown.
If you stand very still, sparrows come
to rest. You know them–the grays
and the browns, one by one.

You learn to call the underworld,
all creatures, and the gods your clan.
You have found your way.
For all that wanders, lost and alone,
then takes a stand, comes at last
to the center.

A STONE
by Jan Lee Ande

From the length of knobbly beach below
St. Michael's By the Sea, I chose a smooth
oval stone, intending to teach it to speak.

I have heard there is a man who lives alone
on an island and he too is loosening such
a voice. His is a wishing stone—black,
banded by one white ring.

My stone is the deepest gray and marly
like a seabird's egg. I warm it between
my palms, calling into being a hollow reed
that might sound notes.

The cobble fairly pulses with consciousness.
I have seen with my own eyes the space
between its atoms, the whole thing quivering
and throbbing—sparks like blue stars flying.

Stories clamor to be told. The stone
sounds its note, fixes its hum. The long
silence recedes.

REDEMPTION
by Jan Lee Ande

All the world is lit with god's light.
It lingers within the lowly places, in the deep
underbelly of things—

In bars where the zealous keep a kind of
communion, their glasses raised.

On misshapen faces, bruised by fists
that leave flowers of flesh (purple, then green)
before fading into memory of muscle and cell.

On the clear drop that trembles at a needle's tip.
In a spent droplet at the head of a shaft.

In poison rain falling on untilled fields.
In the drip and mire of sewage seeping.

In the palsied walk of withered women
making their way over bridges and up alleyways
in Los Angeles and Paris, anywhere at all.

It glimmers in the eye of the atom where
charged particles hurl. And the white cloud
of light bellows the one unknown word.

Contributor

Jan Lee Ande's poetry has appeared in *Iowa Woman, Yellow Silk, Studia Mystica,* and *Nimrod*–for which she was a 1997 Pablo Neruda noted finalist. Poems are forthcoming in the anthology *The Community of Saints* (Story Line Press). She teaches at The Union Institute College of Undergraduate Studies.

A DIALOGUE WITH MY FAVORITE AUTHOR
March, 1961
by Terry Hertzler

The door to the phone booth squeaked
as I closed it carefully
shutting out sounds of traffic
from the street beyond.
Wiping my sweaty hands on my jeans
I unfolded a yellow slip of paper
and stared at the name scribbled there:
James Kjelgaard. Author of *Big Red*, *Haunt Fox*,
Stormy, and *Fire-Hunter*–the finest books
an 11-year-old could imagine.

I stood, dime gripped tightly in my hand
remembering the sudden surge of excitement when
yesterday, having finished his latest masterpiece
I'd read on the inside back cover, "James Kjelgaard
and his wife make their home in Phoenix, Arizona."
Phoenix, Arizona! That's where I live.
James Kjelgaard lives in my town!

And so, trembling inside,
I now stood in the phone booth
afraid to attempt so vital a call from home
the dime hot in my palm, almost slipping
as I dropped it in the slot.
I held my breath as I dialed.
It rang–once, twice.
 "Hello?"
 "Is this James Kjelgaard?"
 "Yes it is."
 "Is this the James Kjelgaard who writes books?"
 "Yes it is."
 "Thank you," I said,
and hung up.

THE NIGHT OF THE DAY THAT DAVEY MAXWELL DIED
by Terry Hertzler

The night of the day that Davey Maxwell died, I sat in the sandy courtyard formed by the five grey hootches of our compound and listened to rock-and-roll songs and watched the moon. The moon was full and bright with the sharp, fragile clarity that is only seen far from cities, a clarity too gentle and serene to have come from the sun–but it had.

The sun. Giver of life, bringer of death. They say the sun kills us, ages us, cuts short the Methuselean span that should be ours. Some say the earth, before the Flood, was sheathed in clouds, clouds that gentled the sun's intemperate gifts and granted long years. But Noah's voyage marked an end to that gift–God's wrath leaving Time ten times more our enemy.

It seemed odd that night, sitting in my chair listening to the Beatles, to feel such peace after seeing Davey die that morning. The music seemed to rise, drawn by the mild night wind, to float above my head before softly drifting off to wherever it is music goes after dancing the tiny bones of our inner ears.

I sat, suspended by a thread that stretched from the past (from a place we called "the World," as if where we were was just an illusion, a dream from which we would soon awake to find ourselves home). I sat clutching that thread, linked to the past through the slowly spinning hubs of my cassette player, enveloped in the familiar cocoon of the music.

My father hated my music, had in fact once smashed my entire collection of 45s, furious that I would buy such trash and hide it in my room. Yet he had sat, patiently–for hours –recording that music, each record, each side, to send to his son in Vietnam. I think I've never loved my father more than when I received those tapes.

Davey never knew his father. His parents were divorced when he was three. He lied about his age to join the Army, had been in-country just two months. He was like some large puppy, friendly and eager, ready to try anything to please. We called him Sunshine.

We were returning from a long, fruitless night reconnaissance, the sun just breaking the horizon, when a single shot knocked Davey to the ground. Our return fire shredded leaves and branches and was swallowed by the jungle. And then silence. For twenty seconds the only sounds were the slight rasps of canvas on cloth, an occasional metallic clink as someone shifted position, the sighs of broken foliage slipping toward the ground, a breath of bluish smoke. Then a bird trilled, and another, and the insects returned and our squad unfroze. Davey lay where he had been thrown by the bullet that tore half his face off. We never found the sniper . . . .

I sat in our compound all night that night playing my tapes again and again, watching the moon slowly cross the sky: beautiful, distant, invincible. The sunrise that morning was the most beautiful I think I've ever seen, the clouds resting like islands above the sea, their colors fiery yet delicate. The sunrise filled me with joy–how strange, the sun.

TOTAL ECLIPSE OF THE MOON
for Rebecca
by Terry Hertzler

Our house is dark and cold. I sit in my car in the driveway. I've opened the sun roof, lowered the seat back, hold binoculars to my eyes and watch darkness slowly glide across the moon's face. There's no hurry. A meteor flashes, bright and gone.

I listen to the radio: *L.A. Woman* by the Doors, *Vincent* by Don McLean. The sky is sharp and cloudless. There's no breeze but November penetrates the layers of shirts and sweaters I wear, and my fingers are numb.

The car shifts as Alice, our butterscotch cat, jumps on the hood, walks up the windshield, pikes her head over the edge of the sun roof. What are you doing? she asks. Why are you here? Her head blocks the sky, disappears.

The moon is dark now, a shadow rimmed in red, remnants of reflected light, penumbral illusion of an illusion. Things align and unalign: the earth, sun, moon–you & me.

I watch the moon, hold binoculars to my eyes, wait. Even though my arms are braced and my breathing is slow and calm, the image jumps each time my heart beats.

Contributor

Terry Hertzler's poetry and short stories have appeared in a variety of publications (as well as on radio and television), most recently in *Stand Up Poetry: The Anthology* (The University Press, California State University, Press, California State University, Long Beach). His work includes a book of poetry on the war in Vietnam, *The Way of the Snake*, and several "chapbooks" of poetry and fiction. He is currently writing a novel.

TEST

1. What is effective breathing for speech?

2. How can you overcome stage fright?

3. What is the difference between a persuasion and demonstration speech?

4. What makes a good speech?

5. Whom do you know who is a good speaker and why? Please tell me his or her name and what makes this person so good?

6. Do you like your own voice? Is there anything you would like to change about it? Why?

7. What are ethos, pathos and logos?

8. Choose a purpose statement and make an outline:

   - Television entertains children.

   - We should all take a vacation.

   - Everyone needs to learn a second language.

I.a.

  b.

  c.

II.a.

      1.

      2.

  b.

      1.

      2.

  c.

      1.

      2.

III.a.

  b.

  c.

9. How can using your imagination help you to become a better speaker and reader?

10. How can you read with expression?

FINAL CHECKLIST
Remember to...

- Be ready on the right date, at the right time (get there early!)

- Practice, practice, practice.

- Be memorable.

- Stay within the time limit.

- Make an outline with a complete introduction, body and conclusion.

- Have a compelling attention getter.

- Tell the audience the purpose of your speech.

- Relate the topic to the audience.

- Have energy and enthusiasm for your topic.

- Be sincere, believable and organized.

- Hold the audience's attention and interest throughout your speech.

- Make your main points or demonstration clear.

- Explain and prove your points.

- Make your voice clear and easily understood.

- Let the audience feel your commitment to your topic.

- Share eye contact throughout.

- Utilize appropriate hand gestures and facial expressions.

- Stand up straight - shoulders back - head held high.

- Use visual aids when needed.

- Conclude by recapping your purpose and main ideas or demonstration.

- Have an interesting and memorable ending statement.

- Have fun and enjoy.

Good Luck!

Fun Communication Exercises

Bingo 1

Find someone who . . .

hates ice cream	has 6 brothers	loves fried chicken	rides a motorcycle
dances every week-end	has a bicycle	is going to a a wedding soon	likes to sing
takes the bus to school	is married	watches TV every day	likes to eat chocolate
works on a computer often	wants to move to another state	is a great cook	plays soccer

Bingo 2
Find someone who . . .

is happy today	makes Italian food	has 3 children
wants to travel	eats fried tacos	loves swimming
goes out for Chinese food often	has a mustache	likes to bake cookies
listens to classical music	wears glasses	prefers yogurt to ice cream
likes Sylvester Stallone	has change for one dollar	enjoys camping
loves to drive	is a grandmother	likes to shop

Bingo 3
Find someone who . . .

(past tense practice)

ate breakfast this morning	played basketball last week	visited family last weekend	talked on the phone after 7:00 last night
watched TV after 11:30 last night	missed dinner at home last night	watched Spanish TV last night	went to the beach last summer
changed a baby's diaper last week	kissed someone yesterday	wore a short-sleeved shirt to school today	gave someone a birthday gift last week
looked at a magazine last week	brought money to school today	took lunch to school today	stayed home last Saturday night
grew up on a ranch	slept well last night	walked to school today	read the newspaper this morning
wrote a letter last week	bought pizza last week	made soup last week	went dancing last weekend

Bingo 4

Find someone who . . .

(future tense practice)

will read a book today	will listen to the news in English tonight	will buy new earrings this week	will watch TV tonight
will shop for new clothes this week	will drive to the bank today	will talk in English on the telephone tonight	will go fishing this year
will eat ice cream today	will visit a sick friend soon	will speak English today	will drink orange juice today
will do the laundry on Saturday	will wash the car this afternoon	will bring food to school tomorrow	will exercise tomorrow morning
will cook dinner tonight	will do the grocery shopping this week	will go to Tijuana today	will eat tortillas today

Bingo 5

Find someone who . . .

has a young husband	saw children yesterday	has a grand-daughter	has more than 2 nephews
will talk to his father today	has an older husband	saw her mother yesterday	has many relatives
has many aunts	never saw her grandfather	is married for the second time	is an aunt
has many children	has grandsons	likes his brother-in-law	never knew his grandma
has no children	has a lot of cousins	sees neighbors often	wants to have a baby soon

Bingo 6

Find someone who . . .

likes chocolate	has a dog and a cat	has 4 children
knows someone famous	sings in the shower	has bought a Valentine's Day gift
likes school	has been in the hospital	wins in Las Vegas
is going to a party tomorrow	ate pizza this week	hates chocolate
has visited 3 cities in the U.S. outside of San Diego County	has a bank account	likes basketball
has made a long distance phone call recently	likes to swim	made his or her bed this morning
speaks 3 languages	has crazy neighbors	plays a musical instrument

Bingo 7

Find someone who . . .

likes camping	visited Las Vegas in the last 3 months	goes to the movies often	is going out of town next week
is a vegetarian	reads the newspaper every day	likes to play basketball	has a car
has not visited Disneyland	has a birthday in April	sews her own clothes	went to South America
doesn't like to dance	plays chess	has a cat	lived in another state

Bingo 8

Find someone who . . .

is taking 3 classes here	has more than 5 children	lives in a mobile home	speaks 3 languages
plays a musical instrument	likes rock and roll music	goes to the gym 5 days a week	was married in 1998
types 20 words a minute	volunteers at a child's school	was in the hospital for more than 1 day	is going to vote for the next president
is on a sports team	works nights	is in love	cut his or her hair last week

Bingo 9

Find someone who . . .

is always on time for work	likes to work outside	brings lunch to work
works overtime	doesn't like the boss	wants to find another job
loves to work on the computer	was trained for his job	is very busy at work
has a lot of customers at work	likes to work with her hands	enjoys fixing things
has many friends	has a 9-5 shift	needs tools for work

Bingo 10

Find someone who . . .

will not eat turkey on Thursday _____

has a white car _____

likes to cook _____

will make tamales at Christmas _____

made lumpia yesterday _____

has 3 children _____

knows her driver's license number without looking _____

has change for $1.00 _____

wants to be famous _____

is married _____

is single _____

goes to church on Sunday _____

lost his/her keys last week _____

got his/her hair cut last week _____

wants a job _____

likes to dance _____

loves to eat mangoes _____

rides a bicycle _____

has a bike rack on her car _____

takes the bus to school _____

walks to school _____

will go to college _____

has a cat _____

has 2 dogs _____

doesn't like animals _____

is very happy _____

knows how to sew _____

knows 60x65 without writing on paper _____

Bingo 11

Find someone who . . .

(welcome back from Thanksgiving)

went to the grocery store more than 1 time over the vacation _____

played in or saw snow _____

ate too much _____

exercised almost every day _____

was sick _____

visited family more than one time _____

went dancing _____

saw a movie at the theater _____

saw a holiday special on TV _____

spoke English everyday _____

read a book to a child _____

cooked a really big dinner for more than 6 people _____

fixed something in the house (clothes, electrical, plumbing, car, etc.) _____

was sad _____

wrote a letter _____

sang songs _____

had a fight with someone _____

visited a person who she doesn't see often _____

received a special present _____

studied English _____

missed coming to school _____

had a nice dream _____

Tally 1

Get The Facts ! !

Ask 15 people these questions.
Tally (add) the responses

1. What is your favorite kind of cake?

Chocolate   Vanilla   Pineapple   Lemon   Other

2. What color eyes do you like the best?

Brown   Green   Blue   Gray

3. What do you like to do for exercise? (pick one)

Walk   Swim   Run   Play Basketball   Other

4. What sports do you like to watch? (pick one)

Baseball   Soccer   Football   Basketball   Other

5. What food do you like the best?

Burgers   Pizza   Tacos   Hot Dogs   Other

Tally 2

Get The Facts ! !

Ask 15 people these questions.

Tally (add) the responses

1.   What is your favorite kind of music?

Rock 'n Roll   Country   Rap   Classical   Romantic

2.   What is your favorite color?

Red   Blue   Green   Orange   Pink   Other

3.   What do you like to watch on TV?

Soap Operas   Comedy   News   Drama   Cartoons

4.   Where would you like to go on vacation?

Mexico   Hawaii   Florida   Europe   Other

5.   What would you recommend for an 18 year old girl?

Marriage   College   Military   Job   Other

Oh Scrud

"Oh Scrud" is a card game that helps students form words. It develops vocabulary and spelling skills while having fun. You deal out the cards and make words with the letters. There's a discard pile and a pick-up pile. The first one to use all the cards wins. The creators encourage you to use your imagination and make up your own rules.

You can order this game from:

Martin and Associates
110 East Red Shadow Lane
Kanab, Utah 84741

(435) 644-5726   FAX: (435) 644-2012

e-mail: ohscrud@xpressweb.com

Dialogues

Everyone enjoys improving his or her vocal skills which works well when we make our own dialogues. We brainstorm a scenario, figure out who the characters are – their ages, what they look like, what kind of people they are. Then we set the scene and make a script. When the script is finished, you can rehearse and film it. The following is an example of a class script. While the students developed it, everyone was engaged. Everyone wanted to participate and to be involved. It was great to watch the end result. It is fun to cast, rehearse and videotape it. Then you can watch your own classroom movie!

Dialogues:

A Video Script

"At a Club in Ensenada"

- Dialogue 1

Kevin: Hi! What's your name?
Juliet: Why do you want to know?
Kevin: Because you look very interesting.
Juliet: Really?
Kevin: Sure. Do you want to dance?
Juliet: I don't like this song, how about the next one?
Kevin: Ok. Would you like a drink?
Juliet: Yes please.
Kevin: What would you like?
Juliet: A Margarita.
Kevin: Waiter! Please bring one Margarita and one Corona for us.
Juliet: How often do you come here?
Kevin: This is my first time.
Juliet: Me too.
Kevin: Do you like this place?
Juliet: Yes I like it. Do you?
Kevin: Yes. But I don't know anyone here.
Juliet: Now you know me.
Kevin: So, what's your name?
Juliet: My name is Juliet. What's your name?
Kevin: My name is Kevin.
Juliet: Where are you from?
Kevin: Roma.
Juliet: Really? That's so far away. What are you doing here?
Kevin: I'm here on business.
Juliet: What kind of business?
Kevin: The import & export business.
Juliet: What do you buy and sell?

Kevin: Food. The music sounds good. Do you want to dance now?
Juliet: Sure. How long are you going to be here?
Kevin: Two weeks this time. Next time, oh, maybe a month.
Juliet: When's the next time?
Kevin: Next month. What do you do?
Juliet: I am a massage therapist.
Kevin: Are you kidding?
Juliet: No. That's what I do!
Kevin: Can I have an appointment for tomorrow?

(She takes out her appointment book).

Juliet: Let's see, how about Monday at 6:00.
Kevin: Ok. Where do I go?
Juliet: Here is my card with my address.
Kevin: Great!! Do you want to dance again?
Juliet: Sure.

"Still at the Club"

Kevin: Can you tell me some more about you?
Juliet: What do you want to know?
Kevin: Tell me something about your family.
Juliet: I have 2 brothers and 3 sisters.
Kevin: I have one sister and I'm the older.
Juliet: How old is your sister?
Kevin: She's 16.
Juliet: What's her name?
Kevin: Lucia. Do you have a boyfriend?
Juliet: No. I was married, but now I'm divorced. What about you?
Kevin: I'm free now. Do you have any children?
Juliet: No. Thank goodness. Do you?
Kevin: No.
Juliet: Do you like Mexican food?
Kevin: I love it. Do you want to get something to eat?
Juliet: Sure, why not?

"Walking to the Car"

- Dialogue 2

Juliet: Where's your car?
Kevin: Over there!
Juliet: Oh, it's nice!
Kevin: Too bad it's a rental. I have a nicer car in Roma.
Juliet: Oh, really?! What kind of car do you have?
Kevin: I have a black Mercedes convertible.
Juliet: Wow! That's wonderful.

(Kevin opens the car door).

Kevin: Can you suggest a restaurant?
Juliet: Yes. There's one a mile away.
Kevin: Sounds good.

"Inside the car"

- Dialogue 3

Kevin: What kind of music do you like?
Juliet: Slow music.
Kevin: Me too. I have a great tape from Italy.
Juliet: Ok. I would like to hear it.

(He puts the tape on. They listen to some music).

Juliet: I like it. This is nice. Oh, there's the restaurant.

"At the Restaurant"

(They park and go to the restaurant. They sit down).

- Dialogue 4

Kevin: This is a nice place. The food smells good. What do you want to order?
Juliet: Shrimp with rice, what about you?
Kevin: I don't know. What do you recommend?
Juliet: Carne Asada, beans and a green salad.
Kevin: It sounds good.
Kevin: What do you want to drink?
Juliet: Beer.
Kevin: Let's order

(After dinner. Kevin pays the bill. They decide to walk on the beach).

"On the Beach"

- Dialogue 5

Kevin: The night is beautiful, just like you!
Juliet: Thank you. That's so sweet.
Kevin: The weather is a little cold. Do you want my jacket?
Juliet: Please.

(He puts his jacket around her shoulders. They hug and kiss).

"At Lupe's House" *(Next day)*

- Dialogue 6

Carlita: So Lupe, did you get your dress yet?
Lupe: I found one, but I'm not sure. You want to go to check it out with me?
Carlita: Ok. Let's go with Juliet.
Angelica: I have some other plans. You guys go without me.

(The door bell rings, Juliet has arrived. Lupe opens the door).

Lupe: Hi! We were just talking about you. Do you want to come to the mall with us?
Juliet: I'd love to, but I can't. I've go to work tonight.
Lupe: Too bad. Come on out to the pool. That's where we are having breakfast.

"At the Pool"

- Dialogue 7

Carlita: Hi Juliet, Why are you so happy?
Juliet: Last night I met this incredible guy.
Angelica: Congratulations! Finally! Tell us all about him. It's about time.
Lupe: So, what's his name, what does he look like?
Juliet: His name is Kevin and he's handsome. I'll tell you more some other time.

(Juliet's cell phone rings).

Juliet:	Hi, This is Juliet. Who's calling?
Kevin:	It's me, Kevin. What are you up to?
Juliet:	Oh, Kevin! Just having breakfast with my friends.
Carlita:	Is it he?

(Juliet nods her head yes).

Kevin:	Ready for tonight?
Juliet:	Are you?
Kevin:	I'm always ready. So, see you at 6:00.
Juliet:	See you then, Ciao!
Angelica:	So, did he cancel?
Juliet:	Whatever. *(She's angry at Angelica's negativity.)*

(Angelica looks mad).

Lupe:	Should we go to the mall now?
Juliet:	Sorry, I have to go.
Carlita:	I'll go with you Lupe.
Angelica:	I guess I'll see you later guys.

"At the Mall"

- Dialogue 8

Lupe:	Look, that's the one. What do you think?
Carlita:	It looks beautiful. Try it on for me.
Lupe:	Did you see Angelica's face when Juliet got that phone call?
Carlita:	What kind of friend is she?
Lupe:	Jealous.

Impromptu Speaking Topics:

fruits and vegetables	colors	foods
restaurants	books	songs
movie stars	cars	languages
singers/musicians	countries	movies

To Emphasize The Importance Of Listening

I start class by reading a paragraph. Then I ask several questions about it. Many times if learners aren't told to listen, they will just tune out. When they can only answer one out of eight questions, it again brings home the idea that listening is important. Here is a paragraph for you to read:

The auditorium is on the corner of Forest and Cherry Street. It is easily accessible by bus, train or car. It is often used for assemblies during the middle of the week. It can hold up to 580 people comfortably.

There were 362 people in the auditorium last Wednesday. The audience was looking at a panel of speakers who sat on stage in back of the master of ceremonies. He stood in front of a microphone on a stand while introducing the speakers: a housewife, mayor, senator, athlete, school principal, small business owner, and a high school student. Each had his or her own agenda in hand.

Questions:

1. Where is the auditorium located? _____

2. How many people can it hold? _____

3. How many people were in the auditorium last week? _____

4. On what day were they there? _____

5. Who sat on the stage? _____

6. How many speakers were there? _____

7. Where did the master of ceremonies stand? _____

8. What did they have "in hand"? _____

Good listening skills are so important. How many answered all eight questions correctly? Usually it's a low number. What can you do to become a better listener? A group discussion will bring a variety of solutions.

If you are interested in a professional critique, please send a videotaped segment of your speech or literature reading to me. Enclose a check or money order for $50.00 and send to:

Janet Scarpone
Learn Quickly
P.O. Box 336
Boulder, CO 80306-0336

Janet Scarpone received her Master's Degree from Southern Illinois University and began her teaching career there in 1975. She has taught at numerous colleges and universities, including The City College of the City University of New York (CCNY), Rutgers University, Montclair State University, Manhattan Community College, National University, National City Adult School, University of California at San Diego, and the San Diego Community College District. She now teaches at Front Range Community College.

Janet is the recipient of numerous awards and commendations, including the National University Leadership Award, Who's Who Among Young American Professionals, Who's Who of American Women, Who's Who Among American Colleges and Universities, and the 1997 CALCO Excellence in Teaching Award.

She has developed the Learn Quickly Video Series which consists of thirty educational videos and eight workbooks in math, writing, grammar, and oral communication. They are used in hundreds of adult schools, home schools, libraries, and community colleges throughout the country. Because of this system, she had one of the highest and quickest graduation rates while teaching in San Diego County. For more information, please call 1-888-LRN-FAST.